A Fishy Alphabet

in Hawai'i

written by Leslie Ann Hayashi
illustrated by Kathleen Wong Bishop

Mutual Publishing

A Angelfish

Pretty little angels
floating in the sea,
graced with colors
so heavenly.

A

B Butterflyfish

It looks like it has eyes
on either side.
But the spots are only there
so that it can hide!

A B

C Clownfish

Clowning around,
this fish has a grand time.
It does magic and juggles
and can also rhyme!

A B C

D Dartfish

Fleet fast fish,
colored red, black, and white.
Quick like a dart,
seeing one's a rare sight.

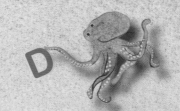

E Eel

The Eel is long
and comes in many hues:
whites, blacks, yellows,
pinks, and blues.

ABCD

F Flounder

This fish is flat
and hides in the sand.
I can't find it.
Maybe you can!

A B C D E

G Goatfish

Known for its beard,
which tickles its chin,
if you haven't seen one,
where have you been?

A B C D E F **G**

H Humuhumunukunukuapua'a

This fish is so small
with a stature so big.
Its long name means
"with a snout like a pig."

A B C D E F G H

'Iao

With a body so small,
and fins the same,
it has large eyes,
but a tiny name.

A B C D E F G H

J Jackfish

We call them Jacks
but they could be Bills,
or maybe even
Sarahs or Jills.

A B C D E F G H I

K Kīkākapu

The Morwong's a referee
with colors of black and white.
Don't question his decision;
he's always right.

ABCDEFGHIJ

L

Lionfish

Quite ferocious,
it lives in the sea.
Be careful to avoid
its territory.

A B C D E F G H I J K L

M Moorish Idol

A Moorish Idol is cool.
Look at that fin!
The black, yellow, and white
make your head spin.

ABCDEFGHIJKL

N Needlefish

Needlefishes are long,
skinny, and thin.
Better watch out!
They could pierce your skin.

N

A B C D E F G H I J K L M

O Onaga

Shining like
a large ruby gem.
They taste really good,
you can also eat them.

ABCDEFGHIJKLMN

P Pufferfish

The Puffer is round
like a basketball.
I suggest you don't bounce it
or throw it at a wall.

A B C D E F G H I J K L M N O

Q Queen Parrotfish

The Queen Parrotfish,
with her crown of greens and blues,
shimmers in the light,
revealing splendid hues.

ABCDEFGHIJKLMNOP

R Rays

With sleek bodies
gliding in the oceans,
Rays move majestically,
with smooth, graceful motions.

ABCDEFGHIJKLMNOPQ

S Squirrelfish

This red and orange fish
looks nothing like a squirrel.
Many vibrant colors
are blended in a whirl.

ABCDEFGHIJKLMNOPQR S

T Trumpetfish

Blowing on their golden horns,
as part of the sea's band,
these long, yellow fish
can't be heard on land.

ABCDEFGHIJKLMNOPQRS

U Unicornfish

In the sea, there's a magical horn
growing on the head of a fish.
No one knows what it's for
but you can still make a wish.

ABCDEFGHIJKLMNOPQRST U

V Velvetfish

This fish looks like
it has a fur coat.
Hard to believe
it can still swim and float!

A B C D E F G H I J K L M N O P Q R S T U

W Wrasse

The Wrasses are some
of the biggest fish in the sea.
A few of them are larger
than even you and me!

ABCDEFGHIJKLMNOPQRSTUV

X

Xyrichtys Pavo

This is a fancy name
for a rather fancy fish.
Without the razor on its head,
it looks just like a dish!

ABCDEFGHIJKLMNOPQRSTUVW

Y

Yellow Tang

This golden yellow fish
looks just like the sun.
You'll be dazzled
the instant you spot one.

ABCDEFGHIJKLMNOPQRSTUVWX

Z

Zebra Rockskipper

A Zebra Fish has many
black and white stripes
which help it to hide
in the coral pipes.

ABCDEFGHIJKLMNOPQRSTUVWXYZ

Help Baby Octopus Find These Alphabet Words Hidden in Each Page

Angelfish, angel, Anemone, anchor, Alan

Butterflyfish, butterfly, Barracuda, bee

Clown fish, circles, coral, Cowry, Cuttle

Dartfish, dart, Damselfish, David, Daniel

Eel, elephant, Emperor Angelfish, Easter egg

Flounder, Flying Fish, flower

Goatfish, Goby, Grasshopper, green

Humuhumunukunukuapuaʻa, Hammerhead Shark, Hermit Crab

ʻIao, insect, island

Jackfish, jellies, Justin

Kīkākapu, key, knot, Kathy

Lionfish, lei, Leslie, Lisa

Moorish Idol, Manini, mosquito

Needlefish, Nautilus, number, necklace

Onaga, orange, 'Opihi, Octopus, ocean

Pufferfish, Pipefish, pineapple, Plumeria

Queen Parrotfish, quadrangle, question mark

Rays, rainbow, rock, Rachel

Squirrelfish, seaweed, Sea Star, Surgeonfish

Trumpetfish, Trunkfish, turtle, trumpet, Taylor

Unicornfish, urchin, umbrella

Velvetfish, Viper Shark, volcano

Wrasse, Wana, White Tip Reef Shark

Xyrichtys Pavo, xylophone, x-ray

Yellow Tang, yacht

Zebra Rockskipper, zucchini

Meet the Author & Illustrator

These two lovely mermaids
met in the first grade.
Since then, they've been friends
and their joy of creating never ends.

Leslie lives by the sea,
in a land called Hawai'i.
She paints, writes,
and dreams at night.

Kathy teaches art
and draws from her heart.
She loves to swim with fishes;
painting fulfills her wishes.

Other Mutual Books by Leslie & Kathy:
Fables From The Deep • Fables Beneath The Rainbow • Aloha 'Oe

Visit Leslie & Kathy at **www.FablesFromTheFriends.com**

Library of Congress Cataloging-in-Publication Data

Hayashi, Leslie Ann.
  A fishy alphabet in Hawaii / by Leslie Ann Hayashi ; illustrated by Kathleen
Wong Bishop.
    p. cm.
  ISBN 1-56647-830-8 (hardcover : alk. paper)
  1. Fishes--Hawaii--Juvenile literature. 2. English language--Alphabet. I. Bishop,
Kathleen Wong, ill. II. Title.
  QL636.5.H3H39 2007
  597.09969--dc22
                        2007013040

ISBN-10: 1-56647-830-8
ISBN-13: 978-1-56647-830-4

Design by Wanni

First Printing, July 2007
1 2 3 4 5 6 7 8 9

Mutual Publishing, LLC
1215 Center Street, Suite 210
Honolulu, Hawai'i 96816
Ph: 808-732-1709 / Fax: 808-734-4094
email: info@mutualpublishing.com
www.mutualpublishing.com

Printed in Taiwan

To Taylor, my poet son,
laureate and super rapper:

Over six feet of fun,
and incredibly dapper.
Thanks for taking the time
to teach me to rhyme.

Love,
Mom

To my daughter Rachel:

You swim through life with
grace, wisdom, and blessings.

All my love,
Kathy